Other works by the author:

Songs and Sonnets
American Cycle:
      U. S. Rivers: Highway 1
      Old California
      Paul Bunyan
      John Henry
      Chief Joseph
      Wyatt Earp
      P. T. Barnum
      Amelia Earhart
      Blue Ridge
      U. S. Rivers: Route 66
White Clouds
Beat Poetry

The Book of Merlin

translated by

Larry Beckett

Livingston Press
The University of West Alabama

Library of Congress Control Number: 2023939866

Typesetting and page layout: Joe Taylor,
Proofreading: Brooke Barger, Savannah Beams

Cover layout and art: Susannah Beckett

The following poems appeared in *The Brazen Head*, an online journal:
Green Warriors, To King Rhydderch, The Bride,
Gwenddydd's Lament, I Decline

The Book of Merlin

Merlin was a 6th-century poet in northwest Britain, who spoke the Brythonic tongue. He was known as Myrddin Wyllt, or Merlin of the Wilds. He was a contemporary and comrade of Taliesin, and though *The Book of Taliesin* is extant, for Merlin, there are only a handful of poems in *The Black Book of Carmarthen*, *The Red Book of Hergest*, and other middle Welsh texts. But scholars have suggested that Merlin's other lyrics were embedded in the Latin poem *Vita Merlini* by Geoffrey of Monmouth. Together, they tell of Merlin's later life. My translation is the first time that his surviving words have been gathered in one manuscript since *The Book of Merlin* was lost in the 12th century.

Contents

Green Commander

Green commander, no lamenting:
let the god guard you from Irish,
on the long hike to the Irish hill,
Franks and Irish not fragmenting.
Aeddan will come, across the wide
ocean; armies from the Isle of Man
will rise with him, from the islands,
the devil's crossroads, spear-quick.

Green commander, no hallooing:
Aeddan will come, across the wide
ocean, and there will be no youth
or tumult, no thunder. He's sallied,
with warriors, weapons, and with
long spears, long lances, has taken
country: let him prosper; and he
has armor, helmets, red swords,
rough boys, a fortress of blood,
fiery horses, and shining shields.
He tells Gwenddydd, at the light
of day, there will be prophecy.
He tells Gwasag, no holding back,
not from home, nor sanctuary.

Green commander, no agonizing:
from troubled air, it's natural to
hear rain. Aeddan will come, with
armies, cross country. Gwenddydd

can't tell what his hands will do:
brothers, in war, burning, won't
be lorded over, not here or there.
I am Merlin, the son of Morfryn,
white hawk, in the awful battle,
when death was joy, arm broken,
and heart's blood, before I'd fly.
Gwenddolau is a memory, and
his companions, and my tragedy
is my death—it comes so slow.

Green commander, listen to me:
it's natural: the lucky are worthy.
Meet Rhydderch, the open hand:
if out of luck, then no deliverance.
I prophesied between deep water
and shallow, since his early attack
on the ships at anchor. Time was
I was in court, in robes of red:
now face and flesh are unlovely,
and to lovely girls I'm invisible.

Green commander, dry your eyes:
to cry's no pleasure, nor for the best.
Merlin will come, his grand designs,
because my brothers, and the king,
Gwenddolau, were killed, Llewelyn,
Gwgon, the open hands, Einion,
Rhiwallon, lord of all the battles.
Meet Rhydderch, treacherous Aeddan,
and it will clang from north to south;
the woods will fill with men at arms.

The Book of Merlin

Green commander, go to sleep:
it's natural to lullaby, natural
for open hands to give, natural
for lovers to love, natural for
men of muscle to hate, but not
for kin to be cold. It's natural
for the commander to be mad,
ravens on corpses, dark spears,
but not for the enemy, under
attack, to care for eye or skull.

Green Warriors

Can doom, so hard, so harm me by
spiriting away all my companions,
who made kings and far kingdoms
shake? We are uncertainty, death
is always here, and it's in power
to strike with its secret blade, blow
poor life out of the body. Green
warriors, who will stand by me
in arms, stave off the commanders
coming to hurt me, and the armies
rising against me? You were brave,
and that bravery has spirited away
all your sweet years, your youth.
Oh only now you were charging
in armor and cutting all of your
enemies down. And now you lie
light on the earth: it's reddening.

Words with Taliesin

I am desolate, now, desolate, now
that Cedfyw is, Cadfan is, fallen.
In fire and tumult, the slaughter,
and the shield shattered, Taliesin.

It was Maelgwn I saw in combat,
and his army hailed him, Merlin.

They lined up in back of two men,
in back of Errith, Gwrrith riding
on a pale horse, on a rackabones,
no doubt, to join up with Elgan,
his death! after his long journey.

And gap-tooth Rhys, his shield
a span, was blessed in battle and,
like Cyndur, killed, unbearable.
Men with open hands are dead,
even the three, Elgan's heroes.

Over and over, more and more,
coming after me, Bran, Melgan,
downing Dywel, in his last battle,
the son of Erbin, and all his boys.

The army of Maelgwn, coming after,
so quick, shining, stood for slaughter.
This battle, Ardderyd—what cause?

all their lives, they've been readying.

An army of spears, a field of blood,
an army of warriors, all mortal,
an army of wounds, an army flying,
an army in retreat from battle.

Seven sons, seven heroes,
seven lances, seven holes.

Seven bonfires, seven armies,
one of seven, always in front.

Seven spears, seven rivers full
of the blood of seven commanders.

Seven score ended: I went crazy,
lost in the woods of Celyddon.
I am Merlin, second only to you,
Taliesin, and I prophesy truth.

To the Apple Tree

Dear apple tree, your branches delight,
luxuriant, shooting, the fruit my fame:
I prophesy to the chieftain of Machrau,
in Machafwy, a Wednesday of blood,
and joy to Lloegyr, and its red blades.
Hello, holy shoat! Thursday's coming,
and the Cymry will rejoice in battle,
defending Cyminod with swordplay,
and the Saxons slaughtered by spears
of ash, and their heads as kickballs.
I prophesy truth: I see a child, rising
out of a shire in the faraway south.

Dear apple tree, luxuriant and green,
your branches big, your shape lovely:
I prophesy tumult, and a frightening
battle at Pengwern, men with mead.
Near Cyminod, he hacks them down,
Eryri commander—only hate's left.

Dear apple tree, now golden, growing
at Tel Ardd, no garden around you:
I prophesy a battle in great Prydein,
defending frontiers against Dubliners.
In seven ships, across the wide waters,
the seven hundred, come to conquer.
Of those that come, only seven will
go back, half empty, as it's foretold.

Dear apple tree, luxuriant, growing,
I once found my food at your foot,
because of a girl, when, with shield
on shoulder, sword on thigh, I slept
all alone in the woods of Celyddon.
Hello, shoat! My words are birds:
kings from over the seas will come
Monday, blessing the Cymry, strong.

Dear apple tree, in the clearing, with
power to hide me from Rhydderch
and his captains, crowding around it,
his army around it, and I'm invisible.
Gwenddydd, with no love or welcome
for me, Gwasag, his ally, with hate
for me: I ruined her son, his daughter.
Death comes to all, but why not me?
After Gwenddolau, no king honors me,
nothing amuses me, no lovely girl
visits me. In the battle of Ardderyd
my regalia was gold, and now I am
despised by the swan white woman.

Dear apple tree, with tender blossoms,
growing in secret in the greenwood:
at daybreak, I heard the story that
Gwasag was offended by my words,
one, two, three times in a day. Ah,
god! if only my end had come before
his blood, her son, was on my hands.

Dear apple tree, by the water,
no servant can eat your wonder.
When I had my reason, I'd lie
at your foot with a sensual girl,
so slim. Fifty years at the whim
of outlaws, I've wandered with
ghosts, no money, no minstrels,
so long, they can't distract me.
Now I can't sleep, shake for my
king Gwenddolau, all my kin.
I'm sick and sad in Celyddon:
at the last end, may I go free.

Dear apple tree, with tender blossoms,
out of the soil of the uneven woods:
the muse has foretold a story, that
a rod of gold, for bravery, will be
given by glorious horse kings, to
the man of grace over the heathen.
For the shining child, bold, Saxons
will fall, and the bards will flourish.

Dear apple tree, red blossom tree,
alive in hiding in Celyddon Wood,
they're looking for your fruit, in vain,
till Cadwaladyr comes from meeting
Cadfaon, by the Twyi shore, the river
Teiwi, anguish out of Aranwynion,
and the wild-haired men are tamed,
comes from meeting at Rhyd Rheon,
Cynan out front, against the Saxons,
the Cymry will win, led by splendor,

all get their rights, the Brythons joy,
and the horns sound, that music, peace.

To the Shoat

Ah, holy shoat, so glad, don't you
go rooting on the top of the hill;
stay down here, hiding in the wood,
away from the dogs of Rhydderch,
the man of faith: I prophesy truth.
As far as Aber Taradyr, in front
of the usurpers of Prydein, all
the Cymry will come under one
commander, Llywelyn, of the line
of Gwynedd, who will overcome.

Ah, holy shoat! We had to run from
the hunters of Mordei, if we dared,
or be followed and caught. If we
go free, I won't say that I'm tired!
I'll predict, from up on the back
of the ninth wave, of the lone white
bearded man who rode Dyfed down,
and who built a sanctuary for doubt,
in the highlands, among the beasts.
Till Cynan comes, nothing's restored.

Ah, holy shoat! I don't sleep easy,
with the tumult of sorrow in me.
I've been suffering for fifty years;
and it's a sorry look that I have.
I saw Gwenddolau, king, in splendor,
gathering plunder, on all his borders;

under the red earth, now, he is so still,
Northern commander, the open hand.

Ah, holy shoat! We had to pray for
fear of the five kings of Normandy;
the fifth coming over the salt sea,
to conquer Ireland, its good towns.
And he made war and chaos, made
red weapons and crying, over there.
And they no doubt will come back
to pay homage at the grave of Dewi.
And I prophesy uproar, and fighting
between the son and father, the land
will know, for the Lloegrians the fall
of their cities, but may they never be
delivered up to the Norman invaders.

Ah, holy shoat! Don't fall asleep;
bad news has come to me, of little
commanders, their words perjury,
and of tight-fisted farmers. When
men in armor come over the sea,
war horses under them, two-faced,
two points on their certain spears,
we'll plow, not reap, world at war,
the grave better than life for poor,
women cuckolds to men's corpses,
and a hard morning in Caer Sallog.

Ah, holy shoat! you pig of peace!
The Sibyl told me a tale of wonder:
I prophesy a summer of fury, in

families, treachery from Gwynedd,
peace long driven out of his land,
seven hundred ships, north wind:
they gather in Aber Deu Gleddyf.

Ah, holy shoat, you blessed animal!
The Sibyl told me a tale of terror:
when Lloegyr quarters in Eiddyn,
in a strong fort in Degannwy, and
clashes with Llywelyn, there'll be
a child chasing, retreat from homes,
when Deinoioel, son of Deinwyn,
is mad. Normans will fly, not ask
the way! At Aber Dulas, seconds
will fail and fall in bloody clothes.

Ah, holy shoat! Pay attention!
A man is starving, god forgives.
The shoat that is alive is mine;
he can go after that that's dead.

Ah, holy shoat! It is bright day.
Listen, waterbirds, loud voices.
For us, the years, the long days,
bad commanders, fruit gone bad.

Ah, holy shoat! with sharp hooves,
get you a mate, when you lie down.
As Rhydderch feasts in Hael hall,
he knows nothing of the sleep I lost,
snow to my knees, in brush like dogs,
icicles in my beard, my way run out.

Tuesday will come, as a day of fury
between warriors, Powys, Gwynedd;
Hirell will rise from his long sleep
to stand against them at the frontier.
And if the god gives me no mercy,
my birth was sorry, my end sorrow.

Ah, holy shoat! It won't be secret,
the army coming from Caerfyrddin,
two whelps leading them with skill,
out of the line of Rhys, commanders
in battle; Saxons dying at Cymerau,
the Cymry's world will be blessed.

Ah, holy shoat! and country animal!
Don't sleep all morning, or burrow
under the hill; Rhydderch and his
hound dogs will come after: before
you make the woods, you'll sweat.

Ah, holy shoat! white and blessed!
The violence I have seen—if you
had seen, you wouldn't run from
desolate lake into the wasteland.
When the Saxons sit Snake Hill,
from a distance, assault Gollwyn,
there'll be brilliant clothes for all.

Ah, holy shoat! Listen, at the hour
the men of Gwynedd give battle,
blades in hand, and horns blowing,
armor will be pierced by spears.

The Book of Merlin

When Normans over the wide sea
come, and the armies clash, great
Prydein will fall to Yswain's sons,
and destruction roll out of London.
And I prophesy two kings who will
make peace from heaven to earth.
Cynan, Cadwaladyr—all Cymry
is where they will meet in praise,
under the laws, out of the troubles,
armies abolished, theft unknown,
deliverance for us, after our trials.
And all take from the open hand.

Ah, holy shoat! on this green mountain,
my beard is grey. Gwenddydd's not here.
When Bernicia's army's come ashore,
the Cymry will win, in a day of glory.

Ah, holy shoat! you're all muscle!
Don't dig a hole, or eat so much,
desire a promise, or love a revel.
I'll give a word to Gwenabwy:
young blood, don't sex around.
I prophesy the battle of Machafwy,
and the red biers on Didmwy Hill,
out of the clash of commanders,
warriors swaggering in saddles,
a morning of sorrow, arriving.
The bear from Deheubarth will rise,
and his justice reach beyond Mynwy.
Gwenddydd's destiny will be blessed,
when the prince of Dyfed dominates.

Ah, holy shoat! The thorn is blossoming,
and the ridge green, the country, beauty.
I prophesy the battle of Coed Llwyfain,
and the red biers, after Owein's attack,
when the seneschals complain so weak,
and there's treachery among the young.
When Cadwaladyr comes to conquer Mon,
the Saxons will be gone from Prydein.

Ah, holy shoat! There will be wonders
in this long country, but I won't care.
When the men who live in Mon come
to claim the Brythons, will be trouble.
And a leader, who lifts spears of light,
strong Cynan, from the banks of Teiwi,
will bring confusion down to Dyfed,
and all of his wealth will be melody.

Ah, holy shoat! It is a wonder:
the world is never long one way.
The Saxons will halloo the cause
to the Brythons, sorrow's heirs.
And I prophesy, before it's over,
Brythons over Saxons: the Picts
say it; the spirit of joy will come
then, that was so long in coming.

Ah, holy shoat! Listen, the stags,
the song of birds by Caer Rheon.
I'm looking up in the mountains
to see the lovely faces, of lovers.

And I prophesy the battle of Iddon,
battle of Machafwy, and of Afon,
battle of Cors Mochno, and of Mon,
battle of Cyminod, and of Caerlleon,
battle of Aber Gwaith, of Ieithion.
When the stags cross Dyfed's border,
a child will rise, good for Brythons.

Ah, holy shoat! There'll be trouble;
it's hard it's coming, but it's coming:
girls will go bare, and wives go loose;
they'll love but they won't reverence;
prosperity won't have an open hand;
and priests will be alien and faithless.

Ah, holy shoat! with little speckles!
Listen to the gulls cry, so strong.
The troubadours, without their due,
stand at the door, empty-handed.
And a wild man from away told me
that strange kings will come, above
the Irish, the Brythons, the Romans,
and they will create chaos and war,
and on Thursday will come to fight
on both of the shores of the Tywi.

Ah, holy shoat! on your thick legs!
Bad guests, a servant in authority,
but losing face, and without honor.
There'll be two brothers, one land,
and out of their claims, long feud.

Ah, holy shoat! There is no point
listening to the gulls, their tumult.
My hair is thin, and my coat cold,
this ditch my barn, but little corn,
my summer store, no help. Before
I break with the incomparable god,
I prophesy: before the world's end,
women not women, men not men.

Ah, holy shoat! how you shake!
My coat is thin; it's not enough.
Since the battle of Ardderyd, I
don't care if sky falls, seas flood.
I prophesy: after Henry, a king
no king, trouble. When there's
a bridge over the Taw, a bridge
over the Tywi, the war will end.

To the Birch Tree

Blessed is the birch, in Wye valley,
branches falling, by ones and twos,
standing till the battle of Ardudwy,
lowing of cattle at Mochnwy Ford,
and spears and yelling at Degannwy,
Edwin at Mon, when he's in sway,
and the green boys, light, fighting,
while their clothes are reddening.

Blessed is the birch, in Pumlumon,
and that will see the stags in fury,
will see the Franks in coats of mail,
at Cefn yr Aelwyd, food for beasts,
and again the monks on horseback.

Blessed is the birch, in Dinwythwy
height, that will know the battle
of Ardudwy, spears at Edryfwy,
a bridge over the Taw, a bridge
over the Tywi, and a frail bridge
on the banks of the Wye: and he
who will build them is Garwy,
in the king of Mon's dominion.
Women under the Danes, men
in torment, are more glad than I,
in waiting, oh but in the time of
Cadwaladyr, they will sing songs.

To the Wolf

Ah god, thou mystery, what can
I do? What place on earth is there
to live? Nothing to eat, no grass
on ground, and no acorns on oak.

Dear wolf, here nineteen apple trees
once stood, holding fruit, now gone.
Who stole them? Where'd they go,
so suddenly? It's now I see them,
now not. Destiny backs, bucks me:
it lets me, and forbids me, to see.

Dear wolf, the apples fail, all else,
the trees, no leaves, no fruit, are my
affliction: I can't cover, can't eat.
Winter, the southern wind, the rains
have taken them. And if I chance
on roots, in deep, the starving pigs
run up and grub them as I dig.

Dear wolf, companion, you once
roved with me through these woods
and clearings; now we can barely
crawl across the field: hard hunger
has weakened us. You've lived here
long before me, and whitened first.
You've nothing to gnaw, amazing,
with all the goats, other animals.

It may be that old age has taken
your strength, and hit your hunt.
All that's left for you is to howl
into the air, as you sprawl, your
skinny body splayed on the earth.

The Seasons

Ah thou mystery, who governs all,
why are the seasons not one, with
four numbers? Spring, by its laws,
is leaf and bud, and summer fruit,
that autumn ripens. Winter, in ice,
is last, and lays the others waste
with rain, and snow oppressing all,
fouling the world by its high winds.
It won't let earth give wildflowers,
the oak acorns, the tree red apples.
If only no winter comes, no frost!

If only spring, summer, the cuckoo
would come back, the nightingale
in solace, with tender air, the dove
in devotion, the birds on branches
in the wildwood, their music, joy,
the bridal earth give the bouquet,
new blossoms in the green grass,
the quiet creeks flow everywhere,
in murmurs, and the blue pigeons,
in a near nest, coo out my lullaby.

The Bride

I can hear Gwendolen grieving,
her tears: I grieve for her, down
in despair. No woman in Wales
of more beauty: beyond goddess,
the blossoms in the hedge, rose
in bloom, the lilies of the field,
in her, only, the light of spring,
in her eyes, only, constellations,
and in the gold glory of her hair.

All this is gone, the grace, away,
the blush, the snow, of her flesh.
She is not what she was, but worn
with crying, she knows nothing of
where her man is, or dead or alive,
and she lies sick, and she is fading,
in the dissolution of the long days.

Gwenddydd is by her side, in tears,
no consolation for her lost brother.
One, by marriage, one, by blood,
devoted, in mourning, pass time,
can't eat, can't sleep: they wander
all night in the wildwood together
with their anxiety burning inside.

To King Rhydderch

Let lords who think that they're poor
have all these gifts, who, not content
with living simply, would have it all.
I'd rather have the oaks, the groves
of Celyddon, high hills, green vales
down below—that's all that I want,
not what you offer, King Rhydderch.
And my wildwood, with all its food,
that I desire over all, will have me.

It's men who pinch pennies, grab
for them, who go for gifts, and they
can be corrupted, so that their wills
can be bent any way they're told.
What they have is not enough, but
for me only the acorns of Celyddon,
the shining creeks, and the grasses.
Let those misers have your bounty,
I can't be bought: give me liberty.

To Queen Gwenddydd

Sister, I don't want her, a cow
that pours out water, so wide,
like the Virgin's Urn in flood.
And my heart won't warp, not
like the singer's, once, the day
his wife had the boys hold her
baskets, before she swam back
across that muddy river, death.

I will keep clear of both of you,
not be destroyed by love. So let
Gwendolen have a chance to wed
whoever she chooses. But let him
take care to keep away from me,
and go another road; he meets me,
and he may get my flaming sword.

But when the holy wedding day
comes, with dishes laid out for
the guests, I'll be there, and I'll
bring true gifts to grace her with
when Gwendolen is given away.

To the Wandering Stars

In the wildwood, and back, I am
a beast; I live on grass, in snow,
in rain, the cruel wind, but this
is better than administering laws
in towns, and ruling over hawks.

Night, and the horns of the moon
luminous, all the lights of heaven
shimmering, and the air so clear,
as the north wind has blown away
the clouds, and withered the mists
with its dry breath, and left the sky
at peace, I watch the planets make
their circles, up on this high hill.

What is that ray from you, Mars?
Does raw red mean a king is dead,
and another's come? I see it's so.
Constantine's died, his kin Conan,
by a bad chance, has murdered his
uncle, and taken the crown, is king.

High Venus, you sail on your way
under the zodiac, and by the sun:
what is that double ray that cuts
across the air? And does that split
foretell the severing of my love?
I see it's so. And we are divided.

I'm gone, and she's abandoned me
for another man, and loves lying
in his arms. I lose her, and he wins.
I wander, and I've lost my rights
to him who's near her skin. I am
not jealous, so let her marry now
it's ripe, cherish him. Tomorrow,
I'll go take her the gift I promised.

To Queen Gwenddydd

Dear sister, why try to hold me?
Not winter with its storms, the cold
north wind roaring in its bad blows,
stinging the flocks with sudden hail,
the south wind filling up the rivers
with rain, can keep me from going
into the wilds, to the green groves.
I only need a little, and I can face
the frost; and in summer, it will be
pleasure to lie in the light coming
through leaves, in the wildflowers.

Ah, food might fail in winter, so
make me a sanctuary; send me
men and handmaidens to serve
me supper when the ground has
no grain, the apple trees, no fruit.
And in front of these buildings,
build one apart, the observatory,
seventy doors, seventy windows,
through which I'll watch the sun
breathe fire, trace Venus, watch
the stars circle all night, that show
what will happen to our country.
Send me scribes, to write down
what I rave, prophecies, on paper.
Dear sister, visit me often, break
my hunger with bread and wine.

Prophecies for Gwenddydd

I've come to you to give you
northern judgement, the beauty
of all dominions I've known.

Since the battle of Ardderyd,
and all that will happen to me,
I'm crazed: where is delight?

I ask my twin, Merlin, who's
druid, diviner; he's ripe for
revelations when a girl goes.

Believe the song of Cadafel,
of the Cymry. The wind says
Rhydderch's flag can't fall.

Now Rhydderch's in glory,
and all the Cymry under:
who will come after him?

Rhydderch Hael, who harried
the warriors, cut them down,
glad day, at the Tawy ford.

While Rhydderch is the enemy
of the town of the bards, in Clyd,
if he goes to the ford, then where?

I'll tell Gwenddydd, sunrise,
as she asks with such skill:
day after tomorrow, he's gone.

I ask my twin, whose fame
is far, who's bold in battle,
who will come after him?

Gwenddolau died in his blood
at Ardderyd, and I've gone wild:
great Morgant, Sadyrnin's son.

I ask my brother, whose fame
is far, who sings among
the streams, who after him?

Gwenddolau died in his blood
at Ardderyd: I'm not invisible?
The country will call on Urien.

Your hair is white as frost,
and the god's given you what
you need: who after him?

Not so, the god's given me
this sorrow; I'm sick at last:
tall Maelgwn, over Gwynedd.

May you live long, dear brother;
my face is sorry with tears:
Maelgwn Hir: who after him?

His name is Rhun, forward
in war, and out in front:
woe to Prydein in his day.

You're slaughter's companion;
men will look to you: Rhun
over Gwynedd: who after him?

He won his name in battle:
what I prophesy will be:
the country in Beli's hands.

I ask my twin, whose fame
is far, who's bold in battle:
hungry Beli: who after him?

My mind's gone—mountain
ghosts: but I go on thinking:
after Beli, his son, Iago.

Your mind's gone—mountain
ghosts: but you go on thinking:
young Iago: who after him?

You come to me with high
brow, at the head of the table:
after Iago, his son, Cadfan.

Your songs have prophesied
fame to the four corners:
new Cadfan: who after him?

Cadwallon, brave: the world
will hear; the Angle's head
will fall, the world admire.

I see the tears on your face,
but I can't help but ask:
Cadwallon: who after him?

The tall man, communing, great
Prydein under one scepter:
the Cymry's best, Cadwaladyr.

Who comes after, so mild,
is weak; what good is he?
After Cadwaladyr, Idwal.

I ask you mildly, whose fame
is far, who's the best man:
mild Idwal: who after him?

After him, in the invincible
way of Dyfafyn, with white
shield, Hywel ap Cadwal.

I ask my twin, whose fame
is far, who's bold in battle:
white Hywel: who after him?

I'll tell you his war stories
before goodbye, Gwenddydd:
after white Hywel, Rhodri.

Cynan will come to Mon
and fail: before the son of
Rhodri, Caeledigan's son.

On behalf of the world,
I ask, for a mild answer:
Cynan: who after him?

Gwenddolau died in his blood
at Ardderyd, and you're afraid:
Merfyn, freckled, from Manaw.

I ask my twin, whose fame
is far, whose song is lucid:
Merfyn: who after him?

Not out of anger, but care, I
say, Prydein under oppression:
after Merfyn, great Rhodri.

I ask my brother, whose fame
is far, who's bold when war
is howling: who after him?

By the shore of the Conway,
in Wednesday's war, they will
honor the tongue of Anarawd.

I ask my brother, whose fame
is far, who's bold to mockers:
old Anarawd: who after him?

The next in line is closer
to the invisible messengers:
the land in Hywel's hand.

The outlanders hold back,
will never get to paradise,
and lay or priest: both bad.

I ask my brother, beloved,
and I hear him celebrated:
outlanders: who after them?

Jabbering barons, a year
and a half, in a short reign:
not careful, and cursed.

You're slaughter's companion;
may there be mercy on you:
the barons: who after them?

One man, out of obscurity,
won't keep honor: Cynan
of the dogs over the Cymry.

On behalf of the world,
I ask, for a mild answer:
Cynan: who after him?

Men from the far countries
will batter down our caers,
and make a baron a king.

On behalf of the world,
I ask; you know the meaning:
the baron: who after him?

I prophesy Serwen, with
white shield, steady messenger,
and stronger than prison.

He will cross the country
of traitors, and they'll be
shaking as far as Prydein.

I ask my brother, blessed,
because it's I who ask:
Serwen: who after him?

Two Belis, with white shields,
will come, and make a tumult:
peace is gold, and will not be.

I ask my twin, whose fame
is far, who's bold in battle:
the Belis: who after them?

A man of passion, whose
counsel is defending, will
come, before the cataclysm.

Who is the man of passion
you prophesy? His name?
What is he? Come when?

His name is Gruffud: fiery,
handsome, and light, he'll rule
over the country of Prydein.

I ask my brother, whose fame
is far, who's bold in battle:
light Gruffud: who after him?

Not out of anger, but care, I
say, Prydein under oppression:
after Gruffud, Gwyn Gwarther.

I ask my brother, whose fame
is far, who's bold when war
is howling: who after him?

Ah, Gwenddydd, the beauty,
the Sibyl told me a tale
of terror, and two brothers.

It's from bad blood, two
brothers, one land, and out
of their claims, long feud.

I ask my twin, whose fame
is far, who's bold in battle:
two brothers: who after them?

I prophesy what no young
man says: a king, a lion,
Gylvin Gevel, wolf's claw.

The Book of Merlin

I ask my deep brother;
I poured mead for him:
Gylvin: who after him?

Compare the number of
his followers to the stars:
the divided Dau Hanner.

I ask my unguarded brother
for the hard key, lord's gain:
divided Dau: who after him?

There'll be a mix of tongues
in battle, Irish and Cymry:
the lord of the eight caers.

I ask my thoughtful brother,
who has read Cado's book:
the lord: who after him?

In answer, he's from Rheged,
the rude king Henry's whelp:
not in his life, deliverance.

I ask my brother, whose fame
is far, who's confident among
the Cymry: who after him?

A bridge over the Taw,
a bridge over the Tywi,
and confusion in Lloegyr.

I prophesy, after Henry's
son, there will come a king
who is no king, and trouble.

I ask my brother, blessed,
because it's I who ask:
no king: who after him?

A king, a fool, will come,
fooled by the men of Lloegyr,
no prosperity under him.

Merlin, beauty, your fame from
song, raging at the world,
what will happen under the fool?

Lloegyr will be moaning,
and Cymry full of sorrow:
the army crossing the land.

Merlin, beauty, whose words
are gifts, don't lie to me:
the army: who after that?

Out of the six, one will
come, who's long hidden,
and he will master Lloegyr.

Merlin, beauty, whose blood
is fame, the wind revolving
in the house: who after that?

Owein will come, conquer
as far as the gates of London,
good news for the Cymry.

Merlin, beauty, who's so gifted,
so famed, I believe your words:
Owein: how long will he last?

Gwenddydd, listen to rumors,
wind whistling in the valley:
five years and two, as before.

I ask my deep brother;
I poured mead for him:
seven: who after that?

When Owein's in Manaw,
battle in Prydein, so near:
a man commanding men.

I ask my deep brother;
I poured mead for him:
battle: who after that?

A man whose upbringing
is good will conquer, and
the country will be joy.

I ask my deep brother;
I poured mead for him:
conquest: who after that?

Outcry in the valley: tall
Beli, his whirlwind men,
bless Cymry, curse Gynt.

I ask my twin, whose fame
is far, who's bold in battle:
tall Beli: who after him?

I prophesy one prince over
Gwynedd, after the troubles,
and with victory over all.

The lord of Morfryn, so united,
Merfyn, and his strong numbers:
before this wish, what happens?

Cadwaladyr lands, big army
Wednesday defending Gwynedd,
and defending Caer Garawedd.

Don't suddenly go, if
you dislike questions: where
will Cadwaladyr land?

In the Tywi Vale, he will
press the Abers; Brythons
will scatter the Brithwyr.

I ask my deep brother;
I poured mead for him:
Cadwaladyr: who after him?

When a fool with three tongues
is in Mon, and his son honored,
they'll say Gwynedd is rich.

Who'll drive Lloegyr back from
the borders? move on Dyved?
And who'll deliver the Cymry?

The rout, the tumult, Rhydderch,
Cadwaladyr's army above the river
Tarddennin, and the key broken.

Don't suddenly go, if
you dislike questions: what
death will take Cadwaladyr?

A spear, from a ship's timber,
in a dark hand, will spit him:
that day disgraces the Cymry.

Don't suddenly go, if
you dislike questions: how
long will Cadawaladyr reign?

Three months, three long
years, full three centuries,
in all the battles, he reigns.

Don't suddenly go, if
you dislike questions:
Cadawaladyr: who after him?

To Gwenddydd I will say,
age after age I'll prophesy:
after Cadwaladyr, Cyndaf.

Hands on the hilts of swords,
and look out for your lives:
with Cyndaf, no white flag.

I ask my deep brother;
I poured mead for him:
Cyndaf: who after him?

The Cymry, no help in battle,
no hope: and from that time,
it's impossible to say.

Ah Gwenddydd, tender beauty,
the first the strongest, Prydein,
and the Cymry will lament.

When killing's the first duty
from sea to land without shore,
woman, the world has ended.

When killing's the first duty,
where's law? Will there be
a circle of stones, a druid?

No druid, and no bard,
no going to the altar,
till heaven falls to earth.

The Book of Merlin

Twin brother, you answer me,
Merlin, son of Morfryn,
the skilled—it's a sad story.

To Gwenddydd I will say,
since you ask it with heart,
woman, there'll be a flood.

I ask my deep brother;
I poured mead for him:
the flood: who after that?

All I prophesied to you,
Gwenddydd, will come
to be, to the last detail.

Twin brother, since it will
happen to me, for our
souls' sake, what king?

Gwenddydd, beauty, courtly,
I will say this with heart:
there will be no more kings.

Sorry, brother, for the cold
separation: after the tumult,
you'll be under the earth.

The airs of heaven will blow
away the air; we'll believe lies,
and prosper till the last day.

Once you dissolve, I poured
mead for you, I will have
nothing: who'll tell the truth?

Out of your hide-out—and read
the book of fire, no fear; listen
to a girl, let your dreams sleep.

Morgenau dead, Morial dead,
Morien dead, cover in battle:
your death, Merlin, is worst.

The god has made me suffer:
Morgenau dead, Morial dead,
Morien dead, all I love dead.

Only brother, don't be harsh:
I'm sick since Ardderyd.
Guide me. I give you to the god.

And I give you to the god
of the living, Gwenddydd,
beauty, the refuge of song.

The songs are standing, in
praise from the four corners:
ah, god! they are so brief.

Gwenddydd, don't you mourn:
the weight's given to the earth.
We must give up what we love.

I live, and won't forsake you,
till the last day, remember:
your blow the hardest of all.

The horse is fast, and the way
easy, bare dark, desolate road:
I go after those who've gone.

I give my innocent brother
to the caer in the clouds:
the god take care of Merlin!

I give my innocent sister
to the caer in the clouds:
the god take care of Gwenddydd.

Prophecies for the Brythons

Ah, Brythons, gone crazy with
opulence! you live in excess:
not satisfied with peace, driven
by furies, to battles between
shires, wars between families,
you let the temples go to ruin,
and drive the holy into exile.

The Boar of Cornwall's kin
throw all into chaos, ambush
and slaughter each other with
their swords, don't wait for
accession, usurp the crown.

But the fourth out of them will
be more harsh, more cruel, till
the sea wolf defeats him, drives
him in defeat across the Severn,
into the wilds, and lays a siege
to Cirencester, and by sparrows
blows down its walls, its houses
down, then sails off to the Gauls
with fleet, dies by a king's spear.

In Leicester, hundreds of monks
will die, Saxons drive out her lord,
leave her empty inside her walls.

Rhydderch will die; after, the Scots
will wrangle with the Cumbrians till
they are given to his growing tusk.

The Cymry will war against Gwent,
after, Cornwall; no law holds them.
They'll force brothers to fight, and to
doom their own kin to a foul death.

The Scots will cross the Humber,
no pity, killing all against them,
but not unpunished, as their lord,
named for a horse, and as animal,
will be killed, his heir driven over
the frontier; the Scots will sheathe
the swords they'd bared too often,
not equal to the strength of Cymry.

Three will wear the diadem: who
after them? The fourth, hurt by his
holier-than-thou, till he crosses, in
his father's clothes, his belt of tusks,
his shadow, the man in the helmet.

Four, by divine right, will vie
for dominion; the two victors
will give and take scepters till
the Gauls are tempted into war.
The sixth will down the Irish,
their walls, and holy and clear-
eyed, revive citizens and cities.

Dun Breatainn will fall, and no
king rebuild it for long years, till
the Boar has overcome the Scots.

Caer Luel will be dispossessed
of its shepherd, be empty, till
the Lion, in strength, restores it.

Caer Sigont and its palace, all its
towers, will be torn down, lament,
till the Cymry come back home.

Ceaster will see its walls broken,
in the harbor, till a man of money
with a wolf's tooth, rebuilds them.

Ruthubi will lie scattered along
the shore, till a man from Flanders,
in a ship with a crest, remakes it.

Mynyw will surrender its walls,
till the fifth from him gives back
the pall that was lost for so long.

Caerleon will drop into your heart,
oh Severn, and lose its citizens, till
the Bear in the Lamb replaces them.

The Saxon kings will drive people
out, hold cities, lands, homes, long,
and three times three dragons will

wear the diadem: who after them?
The first Angle to wear the crown
of old Brutus, in the city empty
by massacre, will bring it to life.
The Danes will come, in a fleet,
defeat us, and reign, short while,
and then be driven out, go back.
Two will rule: the snake forgets
treaties, strikes and stings with
its tail, no garland in its scepter.
The Normans will cross the sea
in ships of wood, face forward,
face back, in iron armor, with
sharp swords, attack the Angles,
kill them, and possess the field.

They will bring kingdoms under, rule
strange nations, till the fury, flying,
drops poison on them. Peace, faith,
honor will go, through the country,
people at war, man betraying man,
and no friend found, husbands not
caring for wives will go to whores,
and wives not caring for husbands
will mate with whoever, no respect
for religion, and the order will die,
the priests in arms, in garrisons, set
up towers and walls on holy ground,
and give what should go to the poor
to troops, carried away by opulence.

Gwenddydd's Lament

Mourn with me, women, mourn
the death of Rhydderch, a man
whose like's unknown on earth,
peace-loving, all those warriors,
no violence, and fair to priests,
with both high and low under
the law, the open hand, giving,
not keeping, all things to all,
doing right, knights' blossom,
kings' glory, kingdom's pillar.

I am in pain, for what he was
is suddenly for worms to eat,
his body in the grave. We had
silk sheets: is this your bed,
your white flesh, king's arms,
covered, under a cold stone,
nothing but dust and bones?
And so it is, our low destiny,
in the long years: none can
go back to what they were.

What use, this glory that comes
and goes, that fools and injures
even the mighty? The bee lays
out honey where it later stings,

like life. The best is brief; this
is its way: like flowing water,
all good passes away. So what
if a rose blush, a lily bloom,
a man, a horse, be handsome?
Questions for the god, not us.

So I'm leaving, all you kings,
high walls, local spirits, dear
sons, all that is of the world.
Today, by my brother's side,
I'll go live in the green wood,
and wrapped in a black shawl,
I'll worship, with a glad heart.

Words of Taliesin

The island of apples is called
The Fortunate Isle, because
it's where all grows by itself,
no need for farmers to plow
the fields, with nature alone
giving the grain, and grapes,
apple trees in the short grass,
springing, spontaneous, and
they live a century or more.

There nine sisters rule those
who come from our country,
and with kind laws. The first
of them in beauty is skilled
in the art of healing, Morgen,
who knows the herbs and how
to cure the body: shape-shifter,
who can fly on strange wings,
to Bristi, Carnoti, Papie, slip
from the sky on to our shore.
She has taught mathematics
to all her sisters, Moronoe,
and Mazoe, Gliten, Glitonea,
and Gliton, Tyronoe, Thitis,
and Thiten, known for the lyre.

Arthur, wounded at the battle
of Camlan, with Barintho at
the helm, who knows the seas
and stars, we made that island;
Morgen took us in with honor,
and in her room, on a gold bed,
uncovered, with her own hand,
his hurt and, looking at it long,
said he could be healed if he
stayed long, and let her work.
So we left him with her, and
spread sail to favoring winds.

Words with Taliesin

Dear companion, since then, what
the country has borne, the oath
broken: it's not what it once was!
By mischance, the men of honor
are fired up, and each is tearing
at the other's vitals. All's upset,
prosperity's gone, what's good.
Citizens, desolate, will abandon
their walls. Saxons, strong in war,
will overthrow us, all our cities,
violate the god's law, his temple.
He'll let this disaster be because—

Then, Merlin, the people should
send off anyone, to tell our leader,
come back, in a quick ship, and if
he's recovered, he can, with his
old vigor, drive off this enemy,
bring the country to its old peace.

No, Taliesin, that's not the way
the invaders will go, once their
claws are in our shores. At first,
they'll conquer us, cities, king,
keep us under by force for years.

Three of us will resist, and with

bravery, end many, overcome,
but incompletely; the Brythons,
weak, will lose their kingdom
for the long years, till Conan
comes wheeling from Brittany,
and Cadwaladyr, the leader of
the Cymry, and they will unite
the men of Scotland, Cumbria,
Cornwall, Brittany in alliance,
give back to the people their
lost crown, drive out enemies,
bring back the days of Brutus,
the cities abiding by old laws.
Kings will go out and conquer
foreign kings again, rule them.

Ah but Merlin, none will then be
left of those who are now living.

Histories for Taliesin

I've lived long years, and seen
many battles, between our own,
and with barbarians, in chaos.

I saw that crime, with Constans
Pendragon betrayed, his little
brothers, Uther and Ambrosius,
across the water. The kingdom,
no leader, was swallowed in war.
Vortigern of Gwent led troops
against all countries for control,
killing the innocent. With quick
violence, he seized the crown,
slaughtered the nobles, and put
the kingdom into submission.

But those allied by blood to
the brothers, offended, set fire
to the cities of this bad luck
prince, assaulted his kingdom
with their harsh armies, and let
him have no chance of peace.
Uneasy, at this rebellion, he
invited men from far nations
so he could face his enemies.

Hordes of soldiers from across

the world were soon in coming
ashore to his welcome, Saxons
sailing in curving keels, troops
in helmets to serve him, led by
the two rough brothers, Horsus
and Hengist, who through hard
duty won over the king. With
the people at odds, the brothers
overwhelmed him, and turned
their blades on them; meeting
with nobles to treat for peace,
they broke their word, in pure
treachery, and murdered them,
driving the prince across the top
of the snowy mountain. All this
I had begun to prophesy to him.

After, the Saxons rode around
burning houses, trying to put
the country under. Vortimer
saw the danger, father driven
out of the hall of Brutus, took
the crown, at the people's will,
attacking the barbarian tribe
oppressing them, many battles,
driving them back to Thanet,
where the fleet was lying that
brought them, and in their flight
the warrior Horsus, many others,
were killed, the king following
and laying siege by land and sea,
in vain, as the enemy, quickly

boarding the galleys, violently
broke free, and made way across
the waters to their own country.

From this victory, Vortimer was
known to the world; he governed
his kingdom with measure. But
the sister of Hengist, Rowena,
couldn't suffer this, and burned.
In the cover of lies, she mixed
up poison in Vortimer's drink
and killed him. She sent word
over the seas to her brother to
cross back with multitudes to
overcome us, and he came with
forces who took booty from all,
and rode around, burning houses.

All this time, Uther and Ambrosius,
in Brittany with their king, Budic,
had lifted swords, and ready for war,
gathered troops, from all the ways,
to go back home, and to drive out
the Saxons wasting their birthright.

So, giving their ships to the wind
and tide, they landed, to be heroes
to their people, drove Vortigern
flying through Wales, caught him
in a tower, and burned it down.

Turning their swords on the Angles,

they met them, in many battles, beat
them, were beaten. At last, in hand-
to-hand, our warriors, at their utmost,
attacked, and giving the enemy deep
losses, and killing Hengist, had won.

After that, the priests and people
gave the crown and kingdom to
Ambrosius. His reign was fair,
but after sixteen years had gone,
he was betrayed by his doctor,
and drinking his poison, he died.

Now his young brother, Uther,
succeeded him, but could not
keep peace: the double Saxons,
always coming back, in their
usual hordes, laid us to waste.
Uther fought in many harsh
battles, and drove them out,
rowing back across the water.

When the campaign was over,
he had peace; a son was born
who was to become majestic,
and in worth, second to none,
his name, Arthur. After Uther
had died, he held the kingdom
for years, in his grief and labor,
with the death of many, in wars.

When Uther lay sick, men with

no faith came from Anglia and
conquered by sword the country
beyond the Humber, as Arthur,
a boy, was too green to defeat
this force. The priests and people
said send to Hoel, the king of
Brittany, tied by blood and love,
bound to help, ask him to come
to uphold us with a quick fleet.

Hoel assembled men from all four
directions for the war, and sailed
to us with thousands, and, joining
with Arthur, he attacked, driving
them back, bad losses. His help
gave Arthur the hope and strength
with his own troops, in charging.
At last, he conquered, forced them
back to their country, and quieted
his kingdom, by law in moderation.

After this war, he soon overcame
the Scots, and changing direction,
the belligerent Irish, all nations,
in all expeditions, the Norwegians,
across the wide waters, the Danes,
he went after with his feared fleet,
and the Gauls, after killing Frollo,
given the country's care by Rome,
and the Romans, out to make war,
when procurator Lucius Hiberius,
the emperor's friend, come by order

of the senate to bring this territory
under control, was killed by Arthur.

The king, desiring to go overseas
and attack his enemies, had given
kingdom and queen into the care
of Mordred, faithless and foolish,
who tried to take the country and
the woman for himself; when word
of this came to Arthur, he set aside
wars, landed home many thousand
men, fighting against his own kin,
drove him flying across the ocean.
The traitor, gathering the Saxons
from all quarters, battled his king,
and, betrayed by his unholy men,
was killed. Such slaughter, sorrow
of women for their sons that day.

The king, wounded to death, left
his kingdom, and sailing across
the water, as you have told, came
to the island of the nine sisters.
Mordred's sons, each out to win
the kingdom for himself, began
wars, each killing his own kin.
Constantine, the king's nephew,
rose against them, harried men
and cities, killing both of them
in a harsh death, took the crown
and ruled the people. Not long,
that peace: his own kin Conan

warred on him, killing the king,
and took the country he governs
weakly, and without intelligence.

Paean

Oh god, through you the machinery
of the skies, the stars, through you
the seas, the land, and its glad seed,
give birth, and feed their offspring,
with their fertility, their profusion,
help us, over and over: through you
all of my delusions have vanished,
and my sanity's come back to me.

I was taken out of myself, and like
a spirit, I knew what we had done,
would do, and the secrets of things,
the flight of birds, the wanderings
of the planets, the gliding of fish.
But all this was vexation to me,
by a hard law, keeping me from
natural rest for my human mind.

Now I have come to myself, and I
am strong with life that had always
flowed in my body. So, dear father
on high, for this I'm grateful, and
I voice full praise, from a full heart,
offering joy. Your generous hand
has reached to me, in two ways, in
a new spring, out of the green grass:
now I have the water I need, and by
drinking from it, my mind is whole.

I Decline

You are young, but at my time
of life, I can't be asked to take
the scepter up, and to be fair.
I'm in old age; it has my body
and slacks my strength; I can
barely walk across the fields.
I have lived long, and enough,
in joy, in abundance, smiling.

In these woods there is an oak,
old and rugged, and so wasted
its sap's failing, and it's rotting.
I saw the acorn as it first fell,
and saw it sprout, woodpecker
above it, on a branch. I saw it
in detail, I honored it, I marked
in memory the place it stands.

I have lived long; age is heavy:
I will not reign again. I'll stay,
green leaves: Celyddon Wood
is my delight, more than corn
of Sicily, grapes of Memphis,
robes in the perfumes of Tyre,
rubies of India, gold of Tagus,
tall towers, or cities in walls.

Nothing can touch me so, or lure
me away from the green woods,
so dear to me, as always. I'll stay
while I'm alive; with its grasses
and its apples, I'll fast and purify,
till I'm worthy of everlasting life.
Look up, the cranes are flying,
in lines, in letters of the alphabet.

The Madman

This madman comes up to us, out
of the blue, or is it destiny, filling
the air with howls, and like a boar,
frothing at the mouth, and clawing
at us. We capture him and sit him
down, and listen, as what he says
will make us laugh. I look closely,
and then I remember who he was,
and sighing, from my heart, I say:

Not how he looked, in our young
years; back then, he was strong,
handsome, and in the blood line
of nobility. He was a companion
in my green days; I was thought
lucky to have friends like this.

One day, out hunting in the high
mountains of Arwystli, we came
to an oak, its branches reaching
into the air. And there, a spring,
rising, in a circle of green grass,
its water good: we were thirsty,
drank deep from the pure stream.
There, apples, fragrant, scattered
in the tender grass, by the shore:
the man who discovered them

gathered and gave them to me,
in his delight at the windfall.
And I handed them out, but left
none for myself, with not enough;
those who got them were smiling,
and said I was generous, and ate
them up, sorry there were so few.

That moment, and a pity to see,
insanity hit this man, the others,
out of their minds, snapping and
clawing like dogs, at each other,
frothing, rolling in the dirt, mad.
Then they ran away, like wolves,
filling the air with howls. I saw,
after, the apples were for me.
In that country was a woman
who'd been attached to me; I
satisfied her, in the long years.
When I swore off her, I would
not live with her, and her desire
was to hurt me, and when all of
her ideas had failed to find any
other way, she set out these gifts,
oiled with poison, by the spring
I'd go by in returning, so I'd find
the apples in the grass, eat them,
and be injured. But chance has
saved me. Have this man drink
from the clear and healing water,
so that if he can recover, he will,
and come to himself. And then he

can labor with me, while his life
lasts, in these groves, for the god.

The lords do this, and the man who
had come raving takes the water,
and recovers, and now recognizes
all of us as his friends, and I say:

You who have in the long years
lived in the wild, like an animal,
no shame, as your mind's back,
don't run from the green groves
you hid in when crazy, but stay
with me; make up for the days
insanity stole from you, serving
the god, who's given you back
the man you are. From now on,
all I have I will share with you,
as long as either of us may live.

And Maeldin answers: Old man,
revered, I don't say no; with joy
I'll be in the green woods with you,
and worship the god with my whole
mind, as long as that spirit controls
my shaking body, for which I will
give my thanks as you guide me.

And Taliesin says: And I will be
the third with you, and turn away
from the whirl of the world; I have
spent long enough living in vain;

now it's time to recover myself,
as you guide me. Lords, go away,
defend your cities; it's not right
to break our peace with all your
words. Enough praise for Merlin.

Prophecies of Gwenddydd

The lords are gone, three left,
Gwenddydd, sister, the fourth;
she once ruled so many, under
the king's law; after his death,
her pleasure is in the woods
with me, in my way of life.
Now, in my hall, looking at
the windows shining in sun,
she says equivocal words
out of her equivocal heart:

I see Oxford filled with men
in helmets, and holy men, by
the council's word, in chains,
men eyeing the shepherd's
tower make him unlock it,
no reason, to his own hurt.
I see Lincoln surrounded by
brute soldiers, two shut in it,
and one escapes, comes back
with a wild tribe, their chief,
and captures the commander,
in a siege, conquers the army.

It's terrible, the stars capture
the sun, and under it, sink
down, not by military force.

I see two moons in the air
near Winchester, two lions,
too fierce, one man looking
at two, and another as many,
face to face, and battle ready.
Others rise up, hit the fourth;
none wins: he stands steady,
holds up a shield, fights back
with weapons, to victory over
the triple enemy. He drives
two across the waste of ice,
and the third, asking mercy,
he gives it, so that the stars
fly away through the fields.

The boar of Brittany, under
its shelter, old oak, takes
away the moon, brandishing
swords behind her back.
I see two stars battling with
wild animals under the hill
of Urien, where the people
of Gwent, of Deira, met in
the reign of old king Coel.
Sweat on skin, and blood
on earth, aliens wounded!
Stars collide; one, falling
into the shadow, hides its
light from light renewed.

It's terrible, the hunger coming,

so that the bellies of the people
will tighten, their bodies empty
of power. It will start in Wales,
go far out through the kingdom,
drive them all across the water.
The calves once living on milk
of cows in Scotland now dying
will go. Normans, get out! quit
bringing your violent soldiers
into our nation; nothing's left
to feed on: you've eaten up all
the mother has made out of her
bounty. May the god help us!
hold back the lions, end wars,
give peace back to the country.

She goes on, and we all listen
in wonder; after a while I go
to her: Sister, does the spirit
move you to foretell? He has
stilled my tongue, and closed
my book. This work is given
to you, rejoice in it, I approve,
and in devotion to him, say all.

Goodbye, Sung out of the Grave

He who's singing out of the grave
says what happens in seven years:
the horse of Eurdein, north, dead.

I've drunk wine from a shining
glass, with awful lords of war:
I am Merlin, the son of Morfryn.

I've drunk wine from a bowl
with the powers, lords of war:
and Merlin is my given name.

When the black wheel, oppression,
comes to destroy weary Lloegyr,
defense will be bitter and long,
the White Mountain see sorrow,
and long regret for the Cymry.

There's no safety in the heights
of Ardudwy, or in the Cymry's
lost ports, from the army's boar.

When the red Norman comes,
his castle at Aber Hodni, there
will be high taxes on Lloegyr,
and even prophecies will cost.

When the man of freckles comes
as far as Ryd Bengarn, men will
face disgrace, hilts break, the new
king of Prydein will be their judge.

When Henri comes to claim
Mur Castell on Eryri's border,
trouble overseas will call him.

When the pale weak man comes
to London, on ugly horses, he
will call out the lords of Caergain.

The acorns few and the corn thick
when a king, young, so sudden
will show and make men shake.

In youth, and big in glory, he
who shoots up a hundred cities:
his life will be tender and frail.

He'll be strong to the weak, weak
to the strong from the high country,
he who comes, bringing dark days.

A time will follow, when whoring
is delight, and women easy victims,
and even girls will need to confess.

A time will follow, when order
is delight, the common do good,
girls will be lovely, boys steady.

The Book of Merlin

A time will follow, at age's end,
when those then young will fail,
and cuckoos die of cold in May.

A time will follow, when dogs
are delight, buildings in hiding;
even a shirt will cost too much.

A time will follow, when cursing
is delight, and sin alive, temples
empty, words and relics, broken,
truth disappearing, lies spreading,
faith weak, and fights abundant.

A time will follow, when clothes
are delight, counsellors vagrants,
bards go empty-handed, priests
smiling, men hated, and denied.

A time will follow, no wind,
no rain, little plowing, less
food, one acre worth nine.

Men will be unmanly, and
corn grow under the trees,
but there will still be feasts.

When trees are honored, there
will be new spring, new king
but bad, barn worse than stake.

On Wednesday, violence, as
blades will wear out, and who
will be bleeding at Cynghen.

In Aber Sor will be a council
of men, after the bad battle,
bright commander in the camp.

In Aber Avon will be the army
of Mon, Angles at Hinwedon,
Moryon's heart in long memory.

In Aber Dwyver the leader will
fail, when Gwidig takes action,
after the battle of Cyvarllug.

At River Byrri will be a battle,
with the Brythons in victory;
Gwhyr's men will be heroes.

In Aber Don will be a battle,
with spears unequal, blood
on the foreheads of Saxons.

Today, you serve, Gwenddydd!
In Aber Carav, the ghosts
of the mountain have told me.

April 2015—July 2016
Portland, Oregon

Sources

The Four Ancient Books of Wales. William Skene,
　　1868
The Vita Merlini. Geoffrey of Monmouth,
　　translated by John Parry, 1925
The Life of Merlin: Vita Merlini. Geoffrey of
　　Monmouth, translated by Basil Clarke, 1973
The Quest for Merlin. Nikolai Tolstoy,
　　contains translations by A. Jarman, 1985
"The Merlin Legend and the Welsh Tradition of
　　Prophecy" A. Jarman, in The Arthur of
　　the Welsh. Edited by Rachel Bromwich,
　　A. Jarman, Brynley Roberts, 1991
Merlin Through the Ages: A Chronological Anthology
　　and Source Book. Edited by R. J. Stewart, John
　　Matthews, 1996
Vita Merlini. Geoffrey of Monmouth,
　　translated by Mark Walker, 2013

Larry Beckett's poetry ranges from songs, *Song to the Siren*, to blank sonnets, *Songs and Sonnets,* to the epic *American Cycle*, including *Paul Bunyan, Wyatt Earp, Amelia Earhart*, and seven other book-length poems. *Beat Poetry* is a study of the poets and poetry of the fifties San Francisco renaissance.

Milton Keynes UK
Ingram Content Group UK Ltd.
UKHW020951071123
432124UK00017B/815